A la Ronde

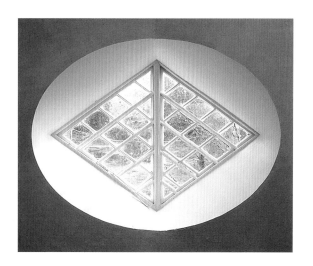

Devon

National Trust

A SIXTEEN-SIDED SPECTACLE

'A curious looking modern building, something between a house and a Temple of a circular shape and with a fantastic chinese looking ornamental roof . . .' is how a bemused visitor to A la Ronde described it in 1866. Twenty years later, another reached an equally unlikely conclusion, when he wrote, 'A la Ronde would not be out of place in one of the South Sea Islands'.

A la Ronde has been a source of fascination to visitors since it was first mentioned in 19th-century guidebooks to Exmouth. The building was constructed in the 1790s and was supposedly inspired by the octagonal basilica of San Vitale at Ravenna. Its creators were two single women, Mary and Jane Parminter, who had been seduced by this Byzantine masterpiece during a ten-year Grand Tour of the Continent at the end of the 18th century. For the next two centuries, the ownership of A la Ronde remained within the Parminter family circle: the Rev. Oswald Reichel (1840–1923) was the only male owner; Margaret Tudor saved it from being sold for development in the 1930s; and Ursula Tudor-Perkins was the last to inherit it in 1973.

In 1935 the descendants of Mary and Jane decided to open the house regularly to visitors. Inevitably, both fabric and furnishings suffered wear and tear, but an even greater threat occurred in 1991, when a planning application was made for permission to build houses on the surrounding garden and fields. Fortunately, with the aid of a grant from the National Heritage Memorial Fund, the National Trust was able to buy the entire property and begin a campaign of long overdue maintenance.

Tree shelter belts have been planted around the perimeter of the estate and footpaths laid. Car-parking has been made less obtrusive and estate railings now surround the drive. The house has been re-roofed, services upgraded and new

accommodation made for staff and visitor facilities. Following research, rooms have been repainted in the colour schemes of the 19th century; furniture too has been restored. Particular attention has been paid to conserving the Parminters' own extraordinary and unique blend of decorative craftsmanship using feathers, shells, paper and paint, besides more unusual materials like sand, moss, seaweed and glass.

The repairs are not yet complete, but A la Ronde can now claim to be the finest example of this particular style of Regency architecture and decoration to survive in Britain.

Above The sixth-century Byzantine basilica of San Vitale at Ravenna

Left A parrot decorated with feathers in the Shell Gallery

Far left A la Ronde today

The Exterior

The site of A la Ronde was carefully chosen to allow a prospect over Exmouth and the sea to the south and east; and towards the Exe Estuary, with the wooded Powderham estate beyond, to the west. Despite the advance of 20th-century suburbs, the views remain remarkably intact. The house sits on a small, raised platform, but this, and other abrupt changes in ground levels, are the only discernible clues to what were once 20 acres of elaborately planted and ornamented pleasure grounds. The original approach to A la Ronde traversed a short drive through diamond-patterned rustic gates. The present route to the car-park is a recent addition.

The external appearance of the house has changed in several respects since it was first built in the 1790s. Late Victorian alterations include the addition of nine dormer windows, following the substitution of tiles for thatch, and the construction of the catwalk. Limewash has been scraped from the limestone walls (although traces can still be seen), and six rectangular windows have been pierced at ground-floor level. Honeysuckle and other climbers on the walls have long since gone. In fact the only distinctive 18th-century features remaining are the sixteen sides of the house, 57.3 metres in circumference, with red-bordered diamond-shaped windows and the green-shuttered sashes perversely fitted at the angles. The cupola and bell were restored in 1996 and three new dovecotes replaced in 2001.

North-east of the house is a long two-storey building, formerly a cob and thatch barn and stables, but faced in brick by the Rev. Oswald Reichel when the north end was converted into a coachman's cottage. Until recently, the front door of the house was linked to the cottage by a Victorian glazed corridor which opened into a conservatory. On the far side of the barn is a brick water-tower, another of Reichel's improvements, the ground floor of which was used as a wash-house (partly restored). The barn is now converted to accommodate visitor facilities.

Above Detail of the diamond-shaped windows of A la Ronde

Right The cob and thatch barn and the site of the Victorian conservatory

Middle right Mid-19th-century child's painting of A la Ronde

Far right A la Ronde in the early 19th century; engraving by L.W. Martens

The Hall

You enter at the upper ground-floor level, a fact disguised by the sloping site. This, the main floor of the house, consists of a central octagon (illustrated on the front cover) surrounded by a series of interconnecting principal rooms, roughly rectangular in shape, each originally with a lobby on either side. The Hall is one of the former rooms, entered by a small internal porch. It is also one of four rooms significantly altered by Oswald Reichel, in this case by installing a stained timber staircase in the area of one of the lobbies and piping in part of the massive central-heating system. The effect is to introduce an unexpected dark and Victorian note, which is compounded by the oak furniture that also post-dates the Parminter cousins. The green marbled doors, skirting and window-sill, restored in 1999, are likely to date from Reichel's time. The gas lighting has also been restored.

Pictures and Sculpture

The late 18th-century prints are all contemporary with the house. Several by Francesco Bartolozzi, like other prints at A la Ronde, have been mounted with the black and gold chevron borders that Jane and Mary Parminter favoured. The small bronze statuette on the 17th-century Bible box is of Julius Caesar and the Gallic chieftain Vercingetorix.

The large oil painting portrays the Lyme Mastiff, an enormous dog bred by the Legh family of Lyme Park in Cheshire. The breed is now extinct. At its feet is a papillon.

Furniture

The oak furniture was brought in by Margaret Tudor. A pair of late 18th-century semicircular flower vases on the window-sill is made of tin and decorated with paper patterns cut out and stuck on by the Parminters.

The Study

You bear left into this room where information on the house is available. Originally, this and the adjoining Music Room were used by the Parminter ladies as their bedrooms.

In a case on the wall is one of A la Ronde's treasures, a bedspread coverlet apparently embroidered in the 1750s by relatives of Mary's grandfather, Richard Parminter (1710–72) for his marriage. The bedspread remained at the house until 1970 when it was given to the Victoria & Albert Museum, which has loaned it back to A la Ronde.

The watercolours are part of a loan collection, formed by Eleanor Creeke, depicting east Devon views by the artists John White RA (1851–1933) and Arthur Perry (active 19th century).

The door to the Music Room is the first of a series of doors which once allowed a complete circuit of all ground-floor rooms and lobbies. The doors were designed to slide back into the thickness of the wall, although most have now been altered and some blocked.

Left A section of the seven-feet-square linen coverlet which is embroidered in satin, stem, long and short fern stitches in a variety of coloured silks. Filling stitches include French knots, sheaf and lattice. The background is Italian quilted in backstitch to form an intricate pattern which has been perfectly executed

Far left The Entrance Hall

7

The Music Room

This is one of the seven principal rooms surrounding the Octagon. In this case the Hall is also accessible through yet another door, squeezed into one corner. The room is lit by a large diamond-paned sash-window built on the angle to gain maximum light. There are four similar windows on this floor.

Pictures

Family photographs include a portrait of Reichel (left of the inner door), with colleagues and ordination students at his Oxford theological college (to the right), and his brother-in-law, the Rev. John Tudor (on the mantelpiece).

Among the reproductions of mainly Italian Renaissance religious pictures are amateur paintings by family members, and three etchings by Hedley Fitton (1857–1929), a family friend.

Furnishings

The room is dominated by a walnut boudoir grand piano. It was made by the Knake brothers of Munster in the mid-19th-century. The earlier square piano, dated 1789, is signed by George Gareka, a German piano maker who had workshops in London between 1788 and 1793. To the left of the fireplace the carved oak desk is English, 17th-century.

The Music Room Lobby

The triangular lobby beyond the Music Room has, like its counterparts, a double casement window, also built on the angle, but in the shape of a diamond within an oval splay. These lobbies ingeniously accommodate furnishings in awkward angles with nautical precision. In this case an impression remains of the original paint decoration, with lining-out in pale green, on bookshelves, door panels, a folding table-top and a folding seat to the left of the door.

Pictures

On the window wall is another survival from the Parminter era – a collection of twelve 18th-century family silhouettes with the sitter's identity pencilled beneath each. Both Jane and Mary's portraits are included.

Above The wood and sealskin Inuit models on the mantelpiece were acquired by Ursula Tudor-Perkins's father in Canada

Right The Music Room

The Library

The room is dominated by the mahogany bookcase, in which the break-front overflows with a jumble of Parminter family souvenirs: shells, beadwork, semi-precious stones and votive statues piled on to raked shelving papered with Italian gouaches and prints bought in Switzerland. It is a rare surviving 'cabinet of curiosities', of a type beloved by 18th-century antiquarians. The fireplace opposite is made of black Ashburton marble and on its right are two of Reichel's unmistakable additions: a speaking tube, with a whistle, to the kitchen below and the one remaining radiator in the house, of elephantine proportions. It was heated by a boiler in the basement. Above the window is a precious Parminter relic, a lavishly japanned pelmet.

Pictures

The pictures are a mixture. Above the door, to the right of the window, is a sealed legal document, dated 1791, recording the outcome of a property dispute in favour of Samuel Lavington, a Parminter relation. Over the fireplace is a 17th-century embroidered picture of *The Discovery of the infant Moses*, to the right a stumpwork picture, *Rebecca at the Well*, of similar date, and a landscape embroidered in black silk that once belonged to the Parminters. Above the embroidered picture is an oil portrait of Judge Walrond, and on and near the mantelpiece, silhouettes of Dr Lowder, Joseph and Phillip Hurlock (all Parminter descendants); to the left is an invitation to William IV's coronation in 1830.

In an oval frame above the radiator is an oil portrait of Mary Walrond. Photographs on the radiator shelf include portraits of Reichel in the leather frame and the Rev. John Tudor. The 1880 wedding photograph shows John Tudor and his wife, Stella Reichel, who inherited A la Ronde from her aunts, Jane and Sophia Hurlock.

To the right of the clock are three early views of A la Ronde. The earliest, a lithograph titled *Cottage near Exmouth*, shows the original cupola and rustic front gates and a 19th-century photograph shows the house with thatch and dovecotes.

To the right of the octagon door is the family coat of arms on parchment with the motto *Deo Favente* (God willing).

Books

The books fall into three categories. Those in the large bookcase belonged to the Parminters, those shelved in cases elsewhere to the Rev. Oswald Reichel and his relations. On the Regency bookcase is an exquisite 18th-century library of juvenilia with its collection of miniature school textbooks.

Beyond the Library the characteristic wedge-shaped lobby is now filled by a staircase to the upper floor, inserted in the mid-20th-century.

Take these stairs to the second floor.

Left The tiny 18th-century bookcase in the Library contains a collection of miniature school textbooks

Far left The Library in 1938

The Bedroom

This second-floor room is used as a bedroom. It is one of the eccentricities of the house that originally no rooms at this level enjoyed natural light until Oswald Reichel installed the dormer windows. Apart from making the rooms more habitable, these windows provide sweeping views across the Exe Estuary to Haldon Hill, and towards Exmouth and out to sea. Reichel also had the fireplace fitted and presumably the myriad little cupboards that fill odd angles around the walls. The dumb-waiter machinery, encased behind glass in the far corner, is also evidence of Reichel's Victorian modernisation.

The room has been left furnished as a bedroom, with furniture found by the National Trust in the house.

The Corridor

Through the door to the right is a low corridor hung with oil paintings by Margaret Tudor, the largest of which depicts a vicarage in Berkshire.

A dormer window on the right doubles as a door to the catwalk around the roof. Almost opposite on the left is the flimsy little door to the Shell Gallery. The Gallery is closed to visitors, but television screens, housed in the pantry, provide close-up views of the decoration in this room.

The Dressing Room and Mellows Shell Room

The Dressing Room (formerly a bedroom) has recently been furnished and redecorated by the National Trust in this style. The Shell Room contains a collection of shells donated by Mrs Mellows of London, which is an amalgamation of three 19th-century collections brought from all over the world. The chest-of-drawers dates from the Parminter era.

The Bathroom

Adjacent to the gallery door is a bathroom recently redecorated by the National Trust following the original scheme for the room.

Above Cabinet of shells in the Mellows Room

Right The Dressing Room

Middle right The Bathroom

Far right The Bedroom in 2006 (lampshades since removed)

The Shell Gallery and Staircase

The Shell Gallery and Staircase are the most extraordinary features at A la Ronde, surprising even the most jaded modern visitor despite two centuries of wear and tear. The decoration here and in the Drawing Room is usually regarded as the most accomplished of its kind to have survived in Britain, particularly on this scale.

At A la Ronde, shells, feathers and cut paper were supplemented by lichen, glass, mica, pottery, stones, bones and paint. The Parminter technique was to stick the feathers on card before this was attached to the plaster surface. The shells and other materials were simply pressed into the lime putty skin that covered a coarser pink plaster, before it set.

The two short flights of the narrow staircase which leads up to the Shell Gallery are a Gothic fantasy of painted vaults and pointed arches encrusted with bands of shells on the walls. At the first landing a grotto has been formed around a looking-glass window above a glazed case filled with shells, mirrors, pieces of quartz and quillwork. At the second landing another grotto and glass window have been placed above an elaborate quillwork doll's-house façade. Turning left the stairs open into the Shell Gallery. Above the entrance, the Parminters painted a crown in honour of George III in 1800, and on either side stuck watercolours of birds and shells – the sources of the materials used in the decoration.

Decay and Restoration

The Shell Gallery has suffered damage from both decay and restoration, and one should imagine the walls completely ornamented. The decoration is designed as a zig-zag shell frieze above a clerestory of eight diamond-paned windows (some with their original draught-resistant openings) within shell-encrusted recesses, each with a folding seat. Between the windows are pairs of decorative featherwork panels featuring birds accompanied by moss and twigs, studded at the top with seal impressions. Years of painstaking work were involved in the Gallery's creation, and it will be several years before gentle repair of the entire ensemble can be completed.

The stairs down from the first floor corridor were built for Reichel. They are hung with more prints collected on the Grand Tour. At the bottom are oil portraits of C.P. Reichel, Lord Bishop of Meath, Matilda Hurlock and a large painting of another anonymous Reichel relative.

Retrace your steps through the Hall into the Octagon, and then go straight ahead into the Drawing Room.

Top A window alcove in the Shell Gallery

Above The crown above the entrance to the Shell Gallery was painted by the Parminters in honour of George III in 1800

Left The grotto on the Shell Staircase

Far left The Shell Gallery

The Octagon

Here is the core of the house, from which all the other rooms on the first floor radiate. Most descriptions have exaggerated the Octagon's height, which is in fact 10.7 metres from floor to ceiling; it appears more on account of the attenuated coving to the Gallery. Eight doors lead from it into the seven principal rooms of the house, each with a fanlight and surrounded by an architrave marbled in yellow and green resembling porphyry. There is more marbling on the door rails and uprights, and on the hinged panels sunk into the jambs (which convert into shelves or seats). Very faint remains of what was once Parminter decoupage (cut and pasted paper) are visible in some arch soffits. There is evidence that the Parminters employed marbled finishes in the house but these examples of the craft appear to post-date them.

The Octagon is an unusual room by any standards, but the painted walls are unprecedented. The restoration of the rustic chevron-painted decoration, a scheme probably dating from the Parminters' time, was completed in 1995. It is thought to represent either a seaweed-covered undersea cave lit by the shell grotto above, or perhaps a flame-stitched textile. Evidence of swagged textiles in the coving prompted the National Trust to recreate the tented ceiling in 2002.

Pictures

Opposite the Hall door (to the left) is Richard Parminter, Mary's paternal great-grandfather, and (to his right) John Parminter, Jane's father. Facing them above the Hall door are (to the left) Mary Walrond, née Lavington, maternal grandmother of Mary Parminter, and (to her right) the Rev. John Walrond, her husband. A donation from the Gulbenkian Foundation allowed the portraits to be restored in 1992.

Furniture and Sculpture

The glass globe and 'the dove with extended wings and an olive branch in its beak' suspended from the ceiling and described in Mary Parminter's will have recently been restored and eight of her unique painted hall-chairs also survive.

A late 18th-century mahogany lettered rent-table, supporting a small Parian bust of a classical figure, fills the centre of the room.

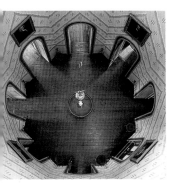

Above The Octagon from the Shell Gallery

Right Mary Parminter's painted hall-chairs have octagonal stringed seats with delicate tapered legs and triangular backs

Far right The recently redecorated central Octagon

The Drawing Room

The labyrinth of small rooms at A la Ronde did not easily satisfy the needs of a Victorian gentleman, but Reichel's solution for creating a drawing room was simple. By removing the lobby between two of the principal rooms he was left with one large room in which he would be comfortable. Fortunately these alterations did not affect the feather frieze and borders, perhaps the most remarkable of the 18th-century decorations in the house.

The contemporary marbled skirting and painted pelmet also survived the Victorian upheaval, and so did one of the original chimney-boards. This was ingeniously designed by the Parminters to comprise a watercolour of St Michael's Mount surrounded by its own seaside collection of shells. They also applied Neo-classical engravings, cut out and stuck on shaped cards, to the overmantel. Reichel's ponderous stained-wood chimneypiece at the opposite end of the room cannot compare with this confection. The room was redecorated in 1999.

Furniture

There are several peculiarly Parminter items in the room as well as contemporary chairs. To the left of the door is an early 19th-century rosewood pedestal jardinière table. To the right of the fireplace is another little painted table, the top of which has been inlaid with semi-precious stones, marble, glass, gems and seals. In the middle of the room there is a similar table, dated 1802, which contains an inner compartment with an engraving of the tomb of Madame Laughans, who died in childbirth.

In the window bay is a rare mahogany-cased mechanical piano, dated approximately 1810 by John Longman and a late 17th-century marquetry inlay longcase clock with the movement signed Pinn of Exmouth (fl.1810–30).

Below The feathers in the frieze in the Drawing Room were culled from native game birds and chickens, then laboriously stuck down with isinglass into a series of concentric circular patterns. In spite of 200 years of light damage from the evening sun and the sometimes less than careful repainting of the walls, the frieze remains largely intact

Bottom The original fireplace in the Drawing Room

Left The Drawing Room

19

Pictures and Objets d'Art

The Drawing Room contains an exceptional number of Parminter works besides pictures collected by them. Left of the door is a rare silhouette and a reverse image of Polly Walrond, Mary Parminter's mother. On the fireplace wall, a little watercolour study of honeysuckle was possibly painted by the same Mary. Beneath it are two pictures of Rome, on skin. The pair of oval 17th-century portraits above the fireplace are Parminter ancestors. Below them are four intricately composed shell pictures in their original frames, made in Italy. On the mantelpiece is a pair of tiny pointed scissors used by the Parminter ladies in cutting out their paperwork pictures. In the alcove to the right, the two Staffordshire pieces are the bequest of Miss Fitt. Both portray conchological subjects.

The photographs on the breakfast table show Oswald Reichel as a child, his brother Lucius, Margaret Tudor, who bought and saved A la Ronde in 1923, and an unidentified cousin.

The pastel portraits either side of the casement window are of Richard Tudor and his wife Joanna, and beneath them, Margaret Tudor to the left and Stella to the right. Below these, on the folding window-shelf table, are two Parminter specialities – a little shellwork figure titled *The Politician*, and a favourite subject for shell artists – a flower display.

The pictures on the fireplace wall are among the most important in the house. They are dominated by the large silhouette group by François Torond (1742–1812), a Huguenot refugee and specialist in drawing with Indian ink. The picture is dated 1783 and shows from left to right: Jane Parminter, her sister Elizabeth, her brother-in-law, George Frend, John Parminter, her brother, and her other sister, Marianne Frend. The silhouettes either side are of Joseph Hurlock and Miss Colville. An early eighteenth-century pencil miniature portrays John Parminter.

Return to the Octagon and turn left into the Dining Room.

Above Large silhouette group by François Torond (1742–1812)

Right A silhouette (with its reverse image) of Polly Walrond, Mary Parminter's mother

The Dining Room and Pantry

This is the only first-floor room, apart from the pantry, that lacks sunshine, perhaps because by the end of the 18th century, dinner, the main meal of the day, was served in the early evening rather than the middle of the afternoon, as had been the custom. The fireplace is a Victorian introduction with tiled slips beneath an imported 17th-century oak overmantel (probably a legacy of Reichel's antiquarian pursuits). The room was redecorated in 1994 following Reichel's paint scheme, which enabled all the marbled finishes on the skirting and doors to be recovered.

Pictures and Furnishings

The dining-table and chairs are late Georgian and there are several indigenous pieces in the room dating from the Parminters' time. They include the following: a tambour-topped sideboard, which has unusual side-opening cellarets, and (left of the fireplace) the oyster kingwood Pembroke table; Piranesi prints from the artist's *Roman Vedute*, and one of Paestum; an oil portrait in the alcove of Sir William Yonge of Escot, Devon; family portraits in silhouette and a group of miniatures, including Mary Parminter (bottom left).

On the overmantel the cut-paper picture with a complex, but so far unexplained, subject and the framed exercise piece in the same medium are both by the Parminters.

The lobby to the left leads to the dumb-waiter connecting with the kitchen. Visitors should leave through the door opposite which enters into the lamp room. The lobby beyond was formerly a scullery and servery, but is now the location for the closed-circuit television. It also provides further information on A la Ronde and an exhibition of a recently donated exotic shell and coral collection. Stairs lead down to the Tea-room and exit. At the base of the stairs there is a shell collection, another introduction. On the top shelf is a miscellany of shells and sea urchins, part of the Mellows Collection. Below are snails from a variety of habitats. At the lowest level are murex shells and a hermit crab.

The Tea-room

Because the first floor was originally unlit beneath the thatch, the servants' bedrooms were here on the south-west side of the ground floor (now used as a flat and not open to the public). To the north and east were service rooms with dumb-waiter access to the Dining Room above, as well as a system of bell and, in the late 19th century, speaking-tube communications.

These rooms included the kitchen, servery, still-room, meat larder and, beneath the Octagon, a wine cellar and strongroom. If the early models and drawings of A la Ronde are correct, natural light in these rooms was limited to only three diamond-shaped windows until Reichel had six rectangular ones added.

The kitchen range is a replacement but the fitted kitchen furniture and the large dresser in the angle of the wall are Victorian. The room was redecorated in 1992 in the original colours of blue and buff.

In the former strongroom two photographs show the meadows surrounding A la Ronde in the 19th century. The contemporary paintings and drawings have been collected by the National Trust. The wine bins contain fragments of glass and china recently excavated from the ha-ha.

Left A la Ronde by Paul Butler, 1987

Above A group of 18th-century miniatures in the Dining Room

THE PARMINTER FAMILY

THE GRAND TOUR

Jane Parminter was the daughter of John Parminter, a Devon merchant from Barnstaple who owned a wine export business in Lisbon, where Jane was born in 1750. Five years later, when the great Lisbon earthquake destroyed the business, John Parminter diversified into the manufacture of a rapid-hardening cement for the rebuilding of the city, and was rewarded by a grateful King Joseph Emanuel, who had a glass factory built for him.

Top Mary Parminter

Above Rebecca Parminter

Jane meanwhile had been sent to London, but her Portuguese childhood seems to have remained a vivid memory. For in 1784, following the death of her father, she decided to embark on a continental voyage accompanied by her invalid sister Elizabeth, an orphaned cousin, Mary, and a London friend, Miss Colville.

The voyage began at Dover on 23 June 1784, and Jane's diaries for the next two months provide a detailed account of the itinerary as far as Dijon. During the first week the four ladies explored Abbeville: 'thirteen bridges, thirteen parishes, thirteen chantries, one handsome cathedral . . . cheap cambric – seven gates, thirteen nunneries . . .' At Chantilly Jane was impressed by the Grand Château of the duc de Condé and especially his cabinet of curiosities, with its 'spar coral, amber, Crystal, Seeds of plants, shells, and many other natural Curiosities'.

The following week the party set off for Paris, which, in common with many contemporary English visitors, they disliked, enduring 'a very dirty Inn indeed, the staircase shaking, the maids bold and impertinent, the treatment sparing and the charge extravagant'. Nevertheless, they persevered with trips to Versailles where they spotted Louis XVI ('a corpulant man not strikingly agreeable') and Marie Antoinette ('tall and elegant small features'). Once again, however, it was the bizarre that appealed, in this case the Royal Menagerie with 'the buffalo, the rhinocerous,

the Pelican, the Panthr [*sic*], African sheep with no tail and a great variety of other things'.

Paris was not neglected by Jane and her companions, and their stamina is briskly illustrated by her record of a single day's sightseeing in the city. They toiled round the church of the Theatines, the Mint, the Grands Augustins, the Carmelite convent, a hospital, another 'old church' (housing a 'black Virgin dresst out in pearls and a number of other baubles'), the Gobelins tapestry factory and the Tuileries gardens. Hardouin-Mansart's Eglise du Dôme at Les Invalides particularly impressed Jane, who thought the plan of the church with its central domed space and satellite chapels, 'A most beautiful church with five domes; the large and middle one represents the 12 Apostles . . . the four corner domes all marble highly enriched . . .' – a distant relative, in fact, of San Vitale at Ravenna.

After a week of this hectic pace the ladies left Paris for Dijon but, frustratingly, Jane's diary ends on reaching the Burgundian countryside. From there they continued south, inspecting Italy, Germany, Switzerland and possibly Spain and Portugal, before returning to England in 1795, where the invalid Elizabeth Parminter died soon afterwards. Nothing daunted, Jane and Mary determined to profit from their experiences by building a new house near Exmouth in Devon, which would remind them of their tour and provide a home for their souvenirs.

The Arms of the Antient Family of the *PARMINTER's* are thus Blazon'd Viz.
An Half Eagle Display'd Or in a Chief Azure. A Salter Gules. with Four Meshes of a Net Voided S. in a Field
Argent. bearing in their Crest an Helmet with in Arm Armed with a Gantlet, holding a broken Sword.
Pommel and Hilt upwards. their Motto Deo Favente. as is above Depicted.

Deo Favente

Above An 18th-century shell
picture which Mary and Jane
purchased on the Grand Tour

Left The Parminter family
coat of arms

ELEGANT EXMOUTH

Exmouth today might seem an unlikely spot for cosmopolitans to settle, but in the 18th century it had developed from being a mere 'fisher townlet' into a fashionable sea-bathing resort, attracting 'some persons of condition'.

Another commentator recommended the town for its climate, which 'though inferior to that of Pisa is, in some respects, like it, by tending to promote insensible persperation [sic]; and from its relaxing quality, always befriending weak lungs'. The views were considered 'as striking in their rural and pastoral loveliness as any which Claude or Gainsborough ever imagined or portrayed.' By the end of the century Exmouth was the most frequented watering place in Devon, and the Rolle family of Bicton, the principal landowners, had begun building suitable houses to accommodate the new residents. They were to include the estranged Viscountess Nelson and Lady Byron, the former prime minister Lord Bute, the poet George Crabbe, Mrs Clarke, mistress of the Duke of York, Sir John Colliton with his collection of rare plants, and Jane's other sister, Marianne, and her husband,

Mr Frend. Early in the 19th century a theatre, a gentleman's club and assembly rooms were added.

The smartest address in Exmouth was The Beacon, where houses were built from 1792 onwards, but instead of moving there Jane built on land outside the town, midway between the two largest neighbouring country houses, Nutwell Court, the newly refurbished home of the Drake family, and Bystock, renowned for its octagonal summer-house paved with 23,000 sheep's hoofs. The site was a good one, about 150 feet above sea level, overlooking Exmouth and the Exe Estuary and facing Lord Courtenay's Powderham estate on the opposite shore.

Below left The Beacon at Exmouth by Henry Haseler 1819

Below right View of Exmouth from the Beacon Walls

Far left View of the Exe estuary from the Shell Gallery

Family tradition maintains that Jane designed A la Ronde herself, but this seems unlikely. One 19th-century writer claimed that it was built 'from plans by a Mr Lowder', which is probably true. Mary Parminter's aunt by marriage, also called Mary, had a sister Anne Glass, who married a Commander John Lowder, a banker. In 1778 the Commander turned to property development and built Lansdowne Place West in fashionable Bath where he lived from 1794, the year before the Parminters bought their site. It may be that his building expertise influenced them sufficiently to suggest the design for A la Ronde. A more plausible theory implicates his son, John Lowder (1781–1829), because he practised as a gentleman-architect in Bath. He was, however, aged only seventeen when A la Ronde was built and is perhaps too young to be considered, although architects were often apprenticed at the age of

fifteen in the 18th century and it was not unknown for them to be designing new buildings at seventeen. Moreover, he was of the same generation as Mary, and brother of Dr William Lowder, who also married into the Parminter family and who is probably the same Dr Lowder who appears in a silhouette in the Library. Furthermore, in 1816 John Lowder designed the Bath & District National School in Bath (demolished in 1896), a 32-sided building with wedge-shaped classrooms similar to the wedge-shaped rooms at A la Ronde. Could it be that A la Ronde was a young man's fancy dashed off for a favoured relation, later to be crystallised in the Bath school?

This evidence seems to support John Lowder's authorship of the house, but whoever was responsible, the extraordinary design points to someone outside the mainstream architectural profession and uninhibited by conventional Regency taste. Moreover, the laborious and intricate decoration of the interiors with feathers, shells and cut paper certainly betrays a delicate feminine touch. It was not uncommon in the 18th century for women to practise the skills of needlework, drawing, japanning, gilding, wood turning and making pictures out of unusual materials, but nowhere have examples of these skills survived in situ in such diversity.

Above A south-facing side of the house

Far right Diamond-shaped windows at A la Ronde

A model of A la Ronde, perhaps by Lucius Reichel, dates from the mid-19th century. It clearly shows the cupola but no windows in the thatched roof and only diamond-shaped windows in the lower ground floor.

Mary Parminter's will contains tantalisingly abbreviated descriptions of the house and its pleasure grounds. For example, it refers to a 'dove with extended wings and an olive branch in its beak suspended over a glass globe' in the Octagon, and two models of the house, one of which still survives as a vital record of A la Ronde's original form. (It is now in the Drawing Room.) The grounds, inhabited by '2 milk cows and 14 sheep', also included an 'obelisk, fountain, shellary, hothouse, greenhouses, sundial, ornamental seats and ornamental gates . . .'

AN UNUSUAL INHERITANCE

Jane died in 1811 and was buried in a tiny chapel which she and Mary Parminter had recently built on a plot of land east of the house. Surrounding the chapel, but under the same roof, were a school and almshouses, and the whole complex was endowed as a charity named 'Point in View'. The charitable purposes were set down in a trust deed which specified that only elderly spinsters could occupy the almshouses and only female children benefit from the education provided, but, and this was the peculiarity of the gift, 'In case of a Jewess who shall ... have embraced Christianity ... she shall be preferred to others.' Although the archaic terms of the trust have been modified and the schoolroom converted into a vestry, the enlarged chapel and its congregation still thrive under the guidance of eight trustees.

In 1849 Mary died, and she too was buried in a vault beneath 'Point in View', leaving a will of extraordinary length, but with two principal aims: to preserve A la Ronde and its contents intact, and to allow only unmarried kinswomen to inherit.

In accordance with the conditions of Mary Parminter's will, two unmarried cousins, Jane and Sophia Hurlock, inherited, followed by their niece, Stella Reichel, a granddaughter of another cousin, Joseph Hurlock. However, changes in property law allowed Stella, by then married to John Tudor, to break the trust and transfer A la Ronde to her brother, the Rev. Oswald Reichel.

A male owner

The Rev. Oswald Reichel has been the only male owner of the house in two hundred years, and during the 1890s he made several fundamental changes in an attempt at modernisation. The thatch was replaced by tiles, the attic converted into rooms lit by new dormer windows and the external catwalk constructed. The Drawing Room was enlarged by removing an internal dividing wall; a new staircase built adjacent to the Hall; additional windows cut into the ground-floor rooms and a central heating system of gargantuan proportions installed.

Reichel, formerly a vice-principal of Cuddesdon College, Oxford, and then a parish priest in Berkshire, lived at A la Ronde from 1886 to 1923, and devoted those years to the study of canon law and antiquarian scholarship. In 1887 he had married Julia Ashenden, who attempted after his death to sell the house for its development potential.

Opening A la Ronde

By chance, a niece, Margaret Tudor, daughter of Stella, saw an advertisement for the property and, with only limited resources, courageously bought it at auction. In 1935 she made another bold move by deciding to open it to the public and it has remained open ever since. During the 1950s the orchard was compulsorily purchased by the local authority for housing and further land sold off in the 1970s in order to finance the property's survival. Margaret died in 1969 and her elderly sister, another Stella, a former actress and pianist (of whom it is said that she 'resembled Ellen Terry but was yet more beautiful') lived on for a further seven years with increasing difficulty, before their first cousin once removed, Ursula Tudor-Perkins inherited in 1973. In 1991 the house, its contents and the remaining 4 hectares (10½ acres) were bought by the National Trust with the help of a grant from the National Heritage Memorial Fund.

Above Oswald Reichel, aged two

Far left The Dining Room prior to redecoration

Left The dove suspended over a glass globe in the Octagon

PARMINTER FAMILY TREE

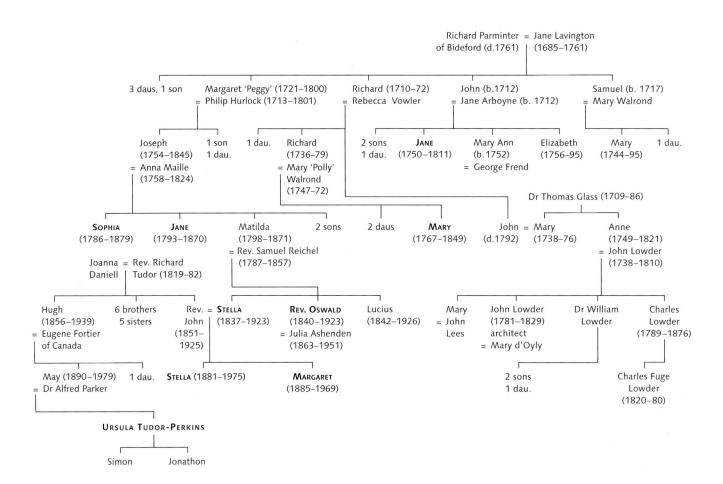

Owners of A la Ronde are shown in CAPITALS